BIBLE STORY

Activity Book
This Book Belongs To:

_____

CONTENTS

The Beginning

In the beginning, God created the heavens and the earth. And God said, "Let there be light," and there was light. God saw that the light was good, and he separated the light from the darkness... And God said, "Let the water under the sky be gathered to one place, and let dry ground appear." Then God said, "Let the land produce vegetation: seed-bearing plants and trees on the land that bear fruit with seed in it, according to their various kinds." God made two great lights—the greater light to govern the day and the lesser light to govern the night... And God said, "Let the water teem with living creatures, and let birds fly above the earth across the vault of the sky." So God created mankind in his own image, in the image of God he created them; male and female he created them. By the seventh day God had finished the work he had been doing; so on the seventh day, he rested from all his work.   –Genesis 1:1,3,4,9,16, 22, 27 2:2

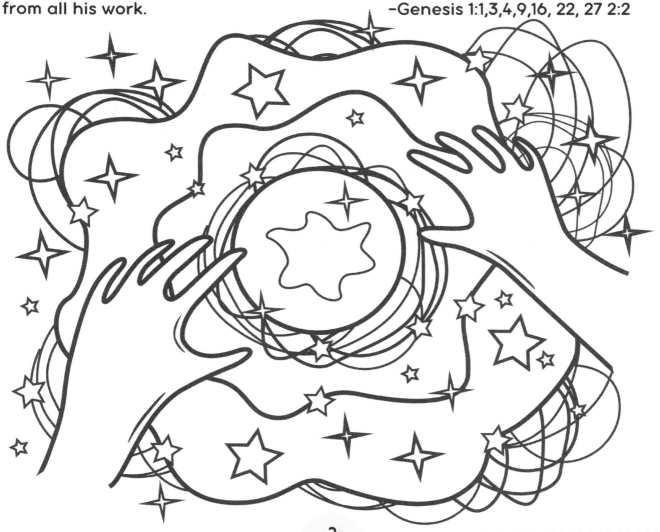

Garden of Eden

Now the Lord God had planted a garden in the east, in Eden; and there he put the man he had formed... The Lord God made all kinds of trees grow out of the ground—trees that were pleasing to the eye and good for food... Now the Lord God had formed out of the ground all the wild animals and all the birds in the sky. The Lord God said, "It is not good for the man to be alone. I will make a helper suitable for him." Then the Lord God made a woman from the rib he had taken out of the man, and he brought her to the man.

– Genesis 2:8,9 2:18,19,22

Noah's Ark

The Lord then said to Noah, "Go into the ark, you and your whole family, because I have found you righteous in this generation. They had with them every wild animal according to its kind, all livestock according to its kind, every creature that moves along the ground according to its kind, and every bird according to its kind, everything with wings. For forty days the flood kept coming on the earth, and as the waters increased they lifted the ark high above the earth. The waters flooded the earth for a hundred and fifty days...Now the springs of the deep and the floodgates of the heavens had been closed, and the rain had stopped falling from the sky. So Noah came out, together with his sons and his wife and his sons' wives. All the animals and all the creatures that move along the ground and all the birds —everything that moves on land–came out of the ark, one kind after another.   Genesis 7:1,14,17,24 – 8:2,18,19

Abraham & Sarah

God also said to Abraham, "As for Sarai your wife, you are no longer to call her Sarai; her name will be Sarah. I will bless her and will surely give you a son by her. I will bless her so that she will be the mother of nations; kings of peoples will come from her." Abraham fell facedown; he laughed and said to himself, "Will a son be born to a man a hundred years old? Will Sarah bear a child at the age of ninety?" And Abraham said to God, "If only Ishmael might live under your blessing!"

– Genesis 17:15–18 (NIV)

Jacob & Esau

Once when Jacob was cooking stew, Esau came in from the field, and he was exhausted. And Esau said to Jacob, "Let me eat some of that red stew, for I am exhausted!" (Therefore his name was called Edom.) Jacob said, "Sell me your birthright now." Esau said, "I am about to die; of what use is a birthright to me?" Jacob said, "Swear to me now." So he swore to him and sold his birthright to Jacob. Then Jacob gave Esau bread and lentil stew, and he ate and drank and rose and went his way. Thus Esau despised his birthright.

– Genesis 25:29–34 (NIV)

Joseph's Coat of Many Colors

This is the account of Jacob's family line. Joseph, a young man of seventeen, was tending the flocks with his brothers, the sons of Bilhah and the sons of Zilpah, his father's wives, and he brought their father a bad report about them. Now Israel loved Joseph more than any of his other sons because he had been born to him in his old age, and he made an ornate[a] robe for him. When his brothers saw that their father loved him more than any of them, they hated him and could not speak a kind word to him.

– Genesis 37:2-3-4

Connect the Dots

Moses in the Bulrushes

The woman conceived and bore a son. When she saw that he was a fine child, she hid him for three months. When she could no longer hide him, she took a papyrus basket for him and coated it with tar and with pitch. She put the child in it and laid it in the reeds by the river's bank. Pharaoh's daughter came down to bathe at the river. Her maidens walked along by the riverside. She saw the basket among the reeds and sent her servant to get it. She opened it, and saw the child, and behold, the baby cried. She had compassion on him, and said, "This is one of the Hebrews' children." The child grew, and she brought him to Pharaoh's daughter, and he became her son. She named him Moses, and said, "Because I drew him out of the water."

Exodus 2:2-3-4-5-6   2:10

The 10 Plagues

Then the Lord said to Moses, "Get up early in the morning, confront Pharaoh and say to him, 'This is what the Lord, the God of the Hebrews, says: Let my people go, so that they may worship me, or this time I will send the full force of my plagues against you and against your officials and your people, so you may know that there is no one like me in all the earth. For by now I could have stretched out my hand and struck you and your people with a plague that would have wiped you off the earth. But I have raised you up[a] for this very purpose, that I might show you my power and that my name might be proclaimed in all the earth. You still set yourself against my people and will not let them go. Therefore, at this time tomorrow I will send the worst hailstorm that has ever fallen on Egypt, from the day it was founded till now.

Exodus 9:13-18 (NIV)

The 10 Plagues

 1 – The Nile River turned to blood.

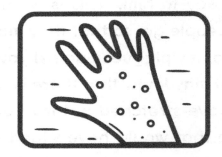 6 – The people were covered in boils.

 2 – Frogs were everywhere.

 7 – A hail storm rained down on Egypt.

 3 – All of the dust became lice.

 8 – Locusts ate all of the trees and plants.

 4 – Flies filled the land and houses.

 9 – Darkness covered the land for 3 days.

 5 – All of the livestock died.

 10 – All first-born sons in Egypt died.

Connect the Dots

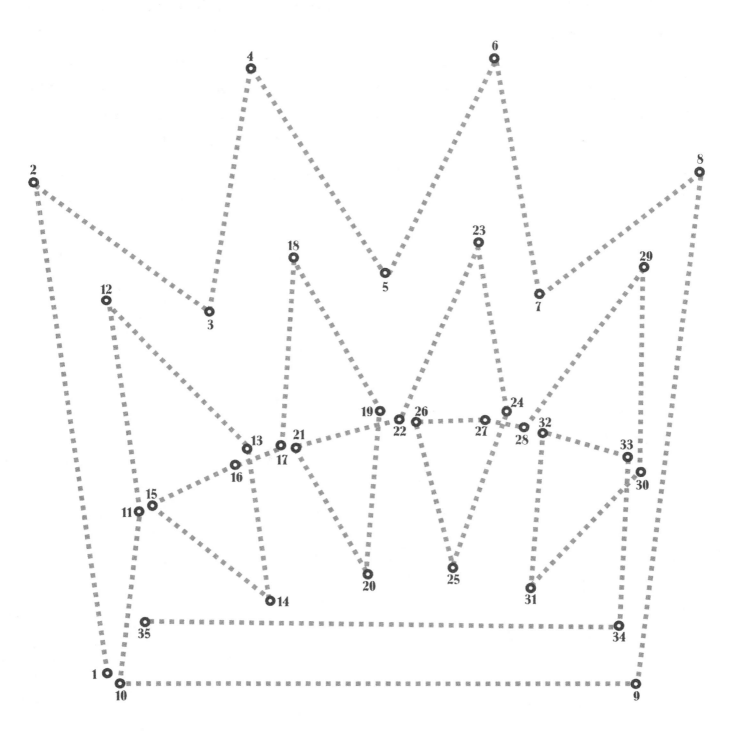

Passover

The Lord said to Moses and Aaron in Egypt, "This month is to be for you the first month, the first month of your year. Tell the whole community of Israel that on the tenth day of this month each man is to take a lamb[a] for his family, one for each household. That same night they are to eat the meat roasted over the fire, along with bitter herbs, and bread made without yeast. "On that same night I will pass through Egypt and strike down every firstborn of both people and animals, and I will bring judgment on all the gods of Egypt. I am the Lord. "This is a day you are to commemorate; for the generations to come, you shall celebrate it as a festival to the Lord—a lasting ordinance. Exodus 12:1-2-3 12:12-14

The 10 Commandments

You shall have no other gods before me.
– Exodus 20:3

You shall not murder.
– Exodus 20:13

You shall not make for yourselves an idol.
– Exodus 20:4

You shall not commit adultery.
– Exodus 20:14

You shall not misuse the name of the Lord your God.
– Exodus 20:7 (NIV)

You shall not steal.
– Exodus 20:15

Remember the Sabbath day, to keep it holy.
– Exodus 20:8

You shall not give false testimony against your neighbor.
– Exodus 20:16

Honor your father and your mother.
– Exodus 20:12

You shall not covet.
– Exodus 20:17

Joshua and the Battle of Jericho

On the seventh day, they got up at daybreak and marched around the city seven times in the same manner, except that on that day they circled the city seven times. The seventh time around, when the priests sounded the trumpet blast, Joshua commanded the army, "Shout! For the Lord has given you the city!

– Joshua 6:15–16 (NIV)

Gideon

During that night the Lord said to Gideon, "Get up, go down against the camp because I am going to give it into your hands. Gideon and the hundred men with him reached the edge of the camp at the beginning of the middle watch, just after they had changed the guard. They blew their trumpets and broke the jars that were in their hands. The three companies blew the trumpets and smashed the jars. Grasping the torches in their left hands and holding in their right hands the trumpets they were to blow, they shouted, "A sword for the Lord and for Gideon!"
Judges 7:9-20-21 (NIV)

Ruth and Naomi

Look," said Naomi, "your sister-in-law is going back to her people and her gods. Go back with her." But Ruth replied, "Don't urge me to leave you or to turn back from you. Where you go I will go, and where you stay I will stay. Your people will be my people and your God my God. Where you die I will die, and there I will be buried. May the Lord deal with me, be it ever so severely, if even death separates you and me." When Naomi realized that Ruth was determined to go with her, she stopped urging her. So Naomi returned from Moab accompanied by Ruth the Moabite, her daughter-in-law, arriving in Bethlehem as the barley harvest was beginning.

– Ruth 1:15-16   1:17-18-22 (NIV)

JOB

After Job had prayed for his friends, the Lord restored his fortunes and gave him twice as much as he had before. All his brothers and sisters and everyone who had known him before came and ate with him in his house. They comforted and consoled him over all the trouble the Lord had brought on him, and each one gave him a piece of silver[a] and a gold ring. After this, Job lived a hundred and forty years; he saw his children and their children to the fourth generation. And so Job died, an old man and full of years.
- Job 42:10-11-16-17 (NIV)

David and Saul

Now the Spirit of the Lord had departed from Saul, and an evil[a] spirit from the Lord tormented him. Saul's attendants said to him, "See, an evil spirit from God is tormenting you. Let our lord command his servants here to search for someone who can play the lyre. He will play when the evil spirit from God comes on you, and you will feel better." So Saul said to his attendants, "Find someone who plays well and bring him to me." David came to Saul and entered his service. Saul liked him very much, and David became one of his armor-bearers. Whenever the spirit from God came on Saul, David would take up his lyre and play. Then relief would come to Saul; he would feel better, and the evil spirit would leave him.

1 Samuel 14:15:16:17:21:23

David and Goliath

Then David said to the Philistine, "You come to me with a sword, with a spear, and with a javelin; but I come to you in the name of Yahweh of Armies, the God of the armies of Israel, whom you have defied. David put his hand in his bag, took a stone and slung it, and struck the Philistine in his forehead. The stone sank into his forehead, and he fell on his face to the earth.
1 Samuel 17:45,49

Elijah and the Prophets of Baal

At the time of sacrifice, the prophet Elijah stepped forward and prayed: "Lord, the God of Abraham, Isaac, and Israel, let it be known today that you are God in Israel and that I am your servant and have done all these things at your command. Answer me, Lord, answer me, so these people will know that you, Lord, are God and that you are turning their hearts back again." Then the fire of the Lord fell and burned up the sacrifice, the wood, the stones, and the soil, and also licked up the water in the trench. When all the people saw this, they fell prostrate and cried, "The Lord—he is God! The Lord—he is God!"

– 1 Kings 18:36–37–38–39 (NIV)

Elisha the Prophet

Naaman's servants went to him and said, "My father, if the prophet had told you to do some great thing, would you not have done it? How much more, then, when he tells you, 'Wash and be cleansed'!" So he went down and dipped himself in the Jordan seven times, as the man of God had told him, and his flesh was restored and became clean like that of a young boy. Then Naaman and all his attendants went back to the man of God. He stood before him and said, "Now I know that there is no God in all the world except in Israel. So please accept a gift from your servant." The prophet answered, "As surely as the Lord lives, whom I serve, I will not accept a thing." And even though Naaman urged him, he refused.

– 2 Kings 5:13-14-15-16

Color by Numbers

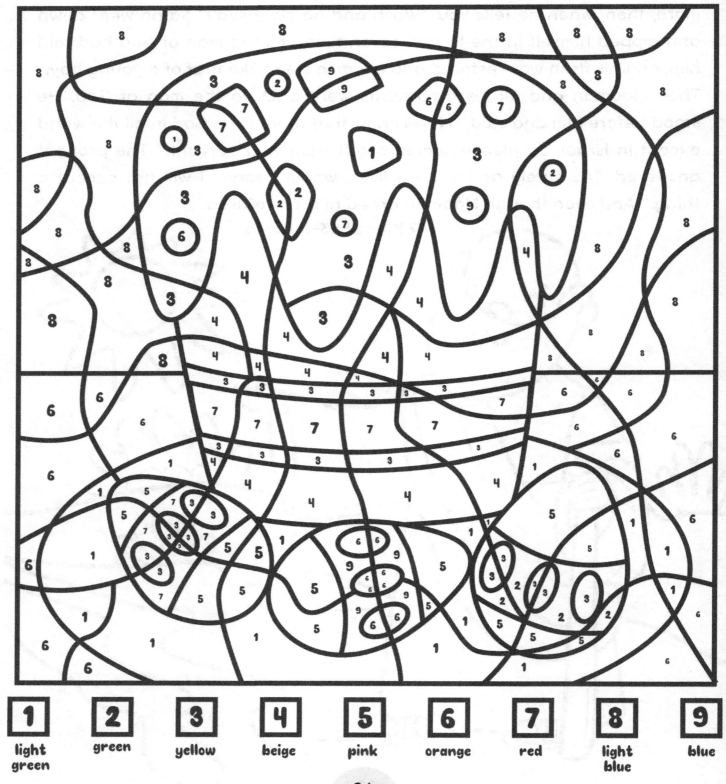

1	**2**	**3**	**4**	**5**	**6**	**7**	**8**	**9**
light green	green	yellow	beige	pink	orange	red	light blue	blue

Jonah and the Whale

Now the Lord provided a huge fish to swallow Jonah, and Jonah was in the belly of the fish for three days and three nights. From inside the fish, Jonah prayed to the Lord his God. He said:

"In my distress, I called to the Lord,
  and he answered me.
From deep in the realm of the dead I called for help,
  and you listened to my cry.
You hurled me into the depths,
  into the very heart of the seas,
  and the currents swirled about me;
all your waves and breakers
  swept over me.

– Jonah 1:17–2:1-2-3 (NIV)

The Nativity Story

For to us a child is born,
    to us a son is given,
    and the government will be on his shoulders.
And he will be called
    Wonderful Counselor, Mighty God,
    Everlasting Father, Prince of Peace.
– Isaiah 9:6(NIV)

Queen Esther

So the king and Haman went to Queen Esther's banquet, and as they were drinking wine on the second day, the king again asked, "Queen Esther, what is your petition? It will be given to you. What is your request? Even up to half the kingdom, it will be granted." Then Queen Esther answered, "If I have found favor with you, Your Majesty, and if it pleases you, grant me my life–this is my petition. And spare my people–this is my request.

– Esther 7:1-2-3

Daniel in the Lions' Den

At the first light of dawn, the king got up and hurried to the lions' den. When he came near the den, he called to Daniel in an anguished voice, "Daniel, servant of the living God, has your God, whom you serve continually, been able to rescue you from the lions?" Daniel answered, "May the king live forever! My God sent his angel, and he shut the mouths of the lions. They have not hurt me, because I was found innocent in his sight. Nor have I ever done any wrong before you, Your Majesty." The king was overjoyed and gave orders to lift Daniel out of the den. And when Daniel was lifted from the den, no wound was found on him, because he had trusted in his God.

– Daniel 6:19-20-21 6:22-23

Unscramble and Match

Unscramble the word, and match it to the picture.

RHCHCU

_ _ _ _ _ _

BELBI

_ _ _ _ _

SORCS

_ _ _ _ _

MINCOMOUN

_ _ _ _ _ _ _ _ _

GEANL

_ _ _ _ _

WNCOR

_ _ _ _ _

The Magi Visit the Messiah

Then Herod called the Magi secretly and found out from them the exact time the star had appeared. He sent them to Bethlehem and said, "Go and search carefully for the child. As soon as you find him, report to me, so that I too may go and worship him." After they had heard the king, they went on their way, and the star they had seen when it rose went ahead of them until it stopped over the place where the child was. When they saw the star, they were overjoyed. On coming to the house, they saw the child with his mother Mary, and they bowed down and worshiped him. Then they opened their treasures and presented him with gifts of gold, frankincense and myrrh. And having been warned in a dream not to go back to Herod, they returned to their country by another route.

– Matthew 2:7–12 (NIV)

Jesus is Baptized

Then Jesus came from Galilee to the Jordan to be baptized by John. But John tried to deter him, saying, "I need to be baptized by you, and do you come to me?" Jesus replied, "Let it be so now; it is proper for us to do this to fulfill all righteousness." Then John consented. As soon as Jesus was baptized, he went up out of the water. At that moment heaven was opened, and he saw the Spirit of God descending like a dove and alighting on him. And a voice from heaven said, "This is my Son, whom I love; with him, I am well pleased."

"– Matthew 3:13–14–15–16–17

Jesus Turns the Water into Wine

Jesus said to them, "Fill the waterpots with water." So they filled them up to the brim. He said to them, "Now draw some out, and take it to the ruler of the feast." So they took it. When the ruler of the feast tasted the water now become wine, and didn't know where it came from (but the servants who had drawn the water knew), the ruler of the feast called the bridegroom and said to him, "Everyone serves the good wine first, and when the guests have drunk freely, then that which is worse. You have kept the good wine until now!"

– John 2:7–10

32

The Beatitudes

Seeing the multitudes, he went up onto the mountain. When he had sat down, his disciples came to him. He opened his mouth and taught them, saying, "Blessed are the poor in spirit, for theirs is the Kingdom of Heaven. Blessed are those who mourn, for they shall be comforted. Blessed are the gentle, for they shall inherit the earth. Blessed are those who hunger and thirst for righteousness, for they shall be filled. Blessed are the merciful, for they shall obtain mercy. Blessed are the pure in heart, for they shall see God. Blessed are the peacemakers, for they shall be called children of God. Blessed are those who have been persecuted for righteousness' sake, for theirs is the Kingdom of Heaven. "Blessed are you when people reproach you, persecute you, and say all kinds of evil against you falsely, for my sake. Rejoice, and be exceedingly glad, for great is your reward in heaven. For that is how they persecuted the prophets who were before you.

– Matthew 5:1–12

The Parables

 The Talents, Matthew 25:14-30

 The Net, Matthew 13:47-50

 The Sower, Luke 8:5-8

 The Pearl, Matthew 13:45-46

 The Lost Coin, Luke 15:8-10

 The Lost Sheep, Luke 15:1-7

 The Wise & Foolish Builders, Matthew 7:24-27

 The Hidden Treasure, Matthew 13:44

 The Budding Fig Tree, Luke 21:29-33

 The Unfair Judge, Luke 18:1-8

Jesus In the Temple

When they did not find him, they went back to Jerusalem to look for him. After three days they found him in the temple courts, sitting among the teachers, listening to them and asking them questions. Everyone who heard him was amazed at his understanding and his answers. When his parents saw him, they were astonished. His mother said to him, "Son, why have you treated us like this? Your father and I have been anxiously searching for you." Why were you searching for me?" he asked. "Didn't you know I had to be in my Father's house?" But they did not understand what he was saying to them. Then he went down to Nazareth with them and was obedient to them. But his mother treasured all these things in her heart. And Jesus grew in wisdom and stature, and in favor with God and man. – Luke 2:45–52

How to Draw Fish

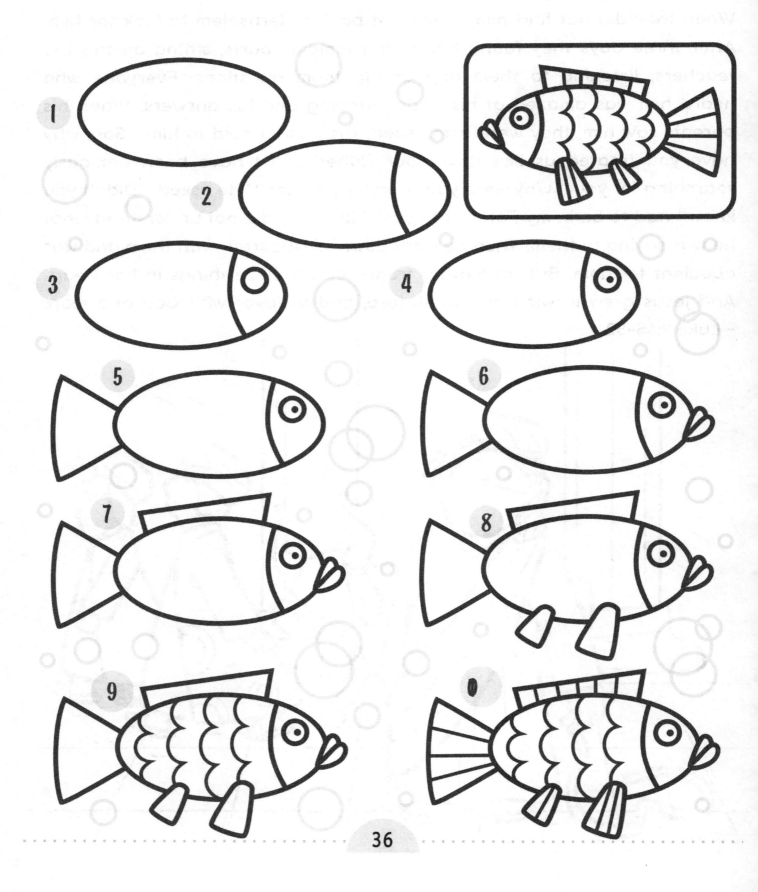

Fisher of Men

When he had finished speaking, he said to Simon, "Put out into deep water, and let down the nets for a catch." Simon answered, "Master, we've worked hard all night and haven't caught anything. But because you say so, I will let down the nets." When they had done so, they caught such a large number of fish that their nets began to break. When they had done so, they caught such a large number of fish that their nets began to break. So they signaled their partners in the other boat to come and help them, and they came and filled both boats so full that they began to sink. When Simon Peter saw this, he fell to Jesus' knees and said, "Go away from me, Lord; I am a sinful man!" He and all his companions were astonished at the catch of fish they had taken.

– Luke 5:4-9

Jesus Feeds the 5,000

He replied, "You give them something to eat." They answered, "We have only five loaves of bread and two fish—unless we go and buy food for all this crowd." (About five thousand men were there.) But he said to his disciples, "Have them sit down in groups of about fifty each." The disciples did so, and everyone sat down. Taking the five loaves and the two fish and looking up to heaven, he gave thanks and broke them. Then he gave them to the disciples to distribute to the people. They all ate and were satisfied, and the disciples picked up twelve basketfuls of broken pieces that were leftover. – Luke 9:13–17

The Good Samaritan

(He) came to him, and bound up his wounds, pouring on oil and wine. He set him on his own animal, brought him to an inn, and took care of him. On the next day, when he departed, he took out two denarii, gave them to the host, and said to him, 'Take care of him. Whatever you spend beyond that, I will repay you when I return.' Now, which of these three do you think seemed to be a neighbor to him who fell among the robbers?" He said, "He who showed mercy on him." Then Jesus said to him, "Go and do likewise."– Luke 10:34–37

The 12 Disciples

"I tell you, whoever publicly acknowledges me before others, the Son of Man will also acknowledge before the angels of God. But whoever disowns me before others will be disowned before the angels of God. And everyone who speaks a word against the Son of Man will be forgiven, but anyone who blasphemes against the Holy Spirit will not be forgiven. "When you are brought before synagogues, rulers and authorities, do not worry about how you will defend yourselves or what you will say, for the Holy Spirit will teach you at that time what you should say."

– Luke 12:8–12

The Parable of the Lost Coin

"Or suppose a woman has ten silver coins and loses one. Doesn't she light a lamp, sweep the house and search carefully until she finds it? And when she finds it, she calls her friends and neighbors together and says, 'Rejoice with me; I have found my lost coin.' In the same way, I tell you, there is rejoicing in the presence of the angels of God over one sinner who repents."

- Luke 15:8-10

The Prodigal Son

Meanwhile, the older son was in the field. When he came near the house, he heard music and dancing. So he called one of the servants and asked him what was going on. 'Your brother has come,' he replied, 'and your father has killed the fattened calf because he has him back safe and sound.' "The older brother became angry and refused to go in. So his father went out and pleaded with him. But he answered his father, 'Look! All these years I've been slaving for you and never disobeyed your orders. Yet you never gave me even a young goat so I could celebrate with my friends. But when this son of yours who has squandered your property with prostitutes comes home, you kill the fattened calf for him!' "'My son,' the father said, 'you are always with me, and everything I have is yours. But we had to celebrate and be glad because this brother of yours was dead and is alive again; he was lost and is found.'"
– Luke 15:25-32

42

Find 7 Differences

Jesus Calms The Storm

A furious squall came up, and the waves broke over the boat so that it was nearly swamped. Jesus was in the stern, sleeping on a cushion. The disciples woke him and said to him, "Teacher, don't you care if we drown?" He awoke, rebuked the wind, and said to the sea, "Peace! Be still!" The wind ceased, and there was a great calm. He said to them, "Why are you so afraid? How is it that you have no faith?" They were greatly afraid, and said to one another, "Who then is this, that even the wind and the sea obey him?"

– Mark 4:37–38   4:39–40–41

Zacchaeus

Jesus entered Jericho and was passing through. A man was there by the name of Zacchaeus; was a chief tax collector and was wealthy. He wanted to see who Jesus was, but because he was short he could not see over the crowd. So he ran ahead and climbed a sycamore-fig tree to see him since Jesus was coming that way. When Jesus reached the spot, he looked up and said to him, "Zacchaeus, come down immediately. I must stay at your house today." So he came down at once and welcomed him gladly...Jesus said to him, "Today salvation has come to this house, because this man, too, is a son of Abraham. For the Son of Man came to seek and to save the lost."
– Luke 19:1-16   19:9-10

Jesus Walks on Water

When evening came, his disciples went down to the lake, where they got into a boat and set off across the lake for Capernaum. By now it was dark, and Jesus had not yet joined them. A strong wind was blowing and the waters grew rough. When they had rowed about three or four miles, they saw Jesus approaching the boat, walking on the water; and they were frightened. But he said to them, "It is I; don't be afraid." Then they were willing to take him into the boat, and immediately the boat reached the shore where they were heading.

– John 6:16–21

Jesus Heals a Blind Man

As he went along, he saw a man blind from birth. His disciples asked him, "Rabbi, who sinned, this man or his parents, that he was born blind?" "Neither this man nor his parents sinned," said Jesus, "but this happened so that the works of God might be displayed in him. As long as it is the day, we must do the works of him who sent me. The night is coming, when no one can work. While I am in the world, I am the light of the world." After saying this, he spits on the ground, made some mud with the saliva, and put it on the man's eyes. "Go," he told him, "wash in the Pool of Siloam" (this word means "Sent"). So the man went and washed, and came home seeing.
– John 9:1–7

Jesus the Good Shepherd

"I am the good shepherd; I know my sheep and my sheep know me– just as the Father knows me and I know the Father–and I lay down my life for the sheep. I have other sheep that are not in this sheep pen. I must bring them also. They too will listen to my voice, and there shall be one flock and one shepherd. The reason my Father loves me is that I lay down my life–only to take it up again. No one takes it from me, but I lay it down of my own accord. I have the authority to lay it down and the authority to take it up again. This command I received from my Father." The Jews who heard these words were again divided. Many of them said, "He is demon-possessed and raving mad. Why listen to him?" But others said, "These are not the sayings of a man possessed by a demon. Can a demon open the eyes of the blind?"

– John 10:14–21 (NIV)

Circle the Excess

Lazarus

Jesus, once more deeply moved, came to the tomb. It was a cave with a stone laid across the entrance. "Take away the stone," he said..."But, Lord," said Martha, the sister of the dead man, "by this time there is a bad odor, for he has been there four days. Then Jesus said, "Did I not tell you that if you believe, you will see the glory of God?" So they took away the stone. Then Jesus looked up and said, "Father, I thank you that you have heard me. I knew that you always hear me, but I said this for the benefit of the people standing here, that they may believe that you sent me." When he had said this, Jesus called in a loud voice, "Lazarus, come out!" The dead man came out, his hands and feet wrapped with strips of linen, and a cloth around his face.   – John 11:38–43

Palm Sunday

The next day the great crowd that had come for the festival heard that Jesus was on his way to Jerusalem. They took palm branches and went out to meet him, shouting,

"Hosanna!"
"Blessed is he who comes in the name of the Lord!"
"Blessed is the king of Israel!"

Jesus found a young donkey and sat on it, as it is written:

"Do not be afraid, Daughter Zion;
    see, your king is coming,
    seated on a donkey's colt."

– John 12:12–15

The 3 Crosses

So the soldiers took charge of Jesus. Carrying his own cross, he went out to the place of the Skull (which in Aramaic is called Golgotha). There they crucified him and with him two others—one on each side and Jesus in the middle. Pilate had a notice prepared and fastened to the cross. It read: Jesus of Nazareth, the king of the Jews. Many of the Jews read this sign, for the place where Jesus was crucified was near the city, and the sign was written in Aramaic, Latin, and Greek. The chief priests of the Jews protested to Pilate, "Do not write 'The King of the Jews,' but that this man claimed to be king of the Jews."   – John 19:16-21

The Resurrection

Becoming terrified, they bowed their faces down to the earth. They said to them, "Why do you seek the living among the dead? He isn't here but is risen. Remember what he told you when he was still in Galilee, saying that the Son of Man must be delivered up into the hands of sinful men and be crucified, and the third day rise again?" They remembered his words, 9 returned from the tomb and told all these things to the eleven and to all the rest.

– Luke 24:5–9

Peter the Healer

"Fellow Israelites, listen to this: Jesus of Nazareth was a man accredited by God to you by miracles, wonders, and signs, which God did among you through him, as you yourselves know. This man was handed over to you by God's deliberate plan and foreknowledge; and you, with the help of wicked men,[d] put him to death by nailing him to the cross. But God raised him from the dead, freeing him from the agony of death because it was impossible for death to keep its hold on him.

– Acts 2:22–24

Solve the Maze

Saul Becomes Paul

As he neared Damascus on his journey, suddenly a light from heaven flashed around him. He fell to the ground and heard a voice say to him, "Saul, Saul, why do you persecute me?"

"Who are you, Lord?" Saul asked.

"I am Jesus, whom you are persecuting," he replied. "Now get up and go into the city, and you will be told what you must do."

The men traveling with Saul stood there speechless; they heard the sound but did not see anyone. Saul got up from the ground, but when he opened his eyes he could see nothing. So they led him by the hand into Damascus. For three days he was blind and did not eat or drink anything.

– Acts 9:3-9

Paul and Silas

About midnight Paul and Silas were praying and singing hymns to God, and the other prisoners were listening to them. Suddenly there was such a violent earthquake that the foundations of the prison were shaken. At once all the prison doors flew open, and everyone's chains came loose. The jailer woke up, and when he saw the prison doors open, he drew his sword and was about to kill himself because he thought the prisoners had escaped. But Paul shouted, "Don't harm yourself! We are all here!" The jailer called for lights, rushed in and fell trembling before Paul and Silas. He then brought them out and asked, "Sirs, what must I do to be saved?" They replied, "Believe in the Lord Jesus, and you will be saved—you and your household."

– Acts 16:25-31

Fruits of the Spirit

But the fruit of the Spirit is love, joy, peace, patience, kindness, goodness, faith, gentleness, and self-control. Against such things there is no law.
– Galatians 5:22–23

Let all that you do be done in love.
– 1 Cor. 16:14

Don't be overcome by evil, but over-come evil with good.
– Rom. 12:21

Rejoice in the Lord always! Again I will say, "Rejoice!"
– Phil. 4:4

Now faith is assur-ance of things hoped for, proof of things not seen.
– Heb. 11:1

Blessed are the peacemakers, for they shall be called children of God.
– Matt. 5:9

A gentle answer turns away wrath, but a harsh word stirs up anger.
– Prov. 15:1

But if we hope for that which we don't see, we wait for it with patience.
– Rom. 8:25

Like a city that is broken down and without walls is a man whose spirit is without restraint.
– Prov. 25:28

The merciful man does good to his own soul, but he who is cruel trou-bles his own flesh.
– Prov. 11:17

For where your treasure is, there your heart will be also.
– Matt. 6:21

Praise to God for a Living Hope

Praise be to the God and Father of our Lord Jesus Christ! In his great mercy, he has given us new birth into a living hope through the resurrection of Jesus Christ from the dead, and into an inheritance that can never perish, spoil or fade. This inheritance is kept in heaven for you, who through faith are shielded by God's power until the coming of the salvation that is ready to be revealed in the last time. In all this, you greatly rejoice, though now for a little while you may have had to suffer grief in all kinds of trials. These have come so that the proven genuineness of your faith–of greater worth than gold, which perishes even though refined by fire–may result in praise, glory, and honor when Jesus Christ is revealed.
1 Peter 1:3–8 (NIV)

Solve the Maze

Find Apples and Count

Find 10 Differences

How to Pray?

Take 1

Dear Father in heaven

How to Pray?

Take 2

Give us this day our daily bread.

Thank You!   **Thank You!**   **Thank You!**

How to Pray?

Take 3

Forgive us our sins as we forgive others...

How to Pray?
Take 4
Lead us not into temptation

How to Pray?

Take 5

Thine is the kingdom and the power and glory forever! Amen

Find and count

Connect the Dots

Find 7 Differences

1. Animals in the Bible

Animals play an essential role in many Bible stories and lessons. Do you remember the dove that brought Noah an olive branch as a sign of peace? Or the great fish that swallowed Jonah? Dive into this word search to find animals that shaped these timeless tales!

```
D  J  L  E  M  A  C  Q  M  F  V  A  Y  J  T
X  X  D  O  N  K  E  Y  C  D  E  E  R  A  H
F  N  L  F  D  O  V  E  Q  Z  N  Z  A  U  Z
H  W  Q  I  C  P  S  T  I  X  Q  L  L  N  H
F  O  L  S  J  E  N  V  D  O  V  B  G  J  N
O  R  D  H  X  W  A  L  C  K  B  S  P  T  F
X  C  C  L  D  S  K  A  O  E  A  G  L  E  Z
O  U  J  L  H  S  E  M  W  G  A  G  F  J  C
W  H  A  L  E  N  M  B  Y  E  U  O  Y  K  I
U  L  I  B  Y  U  S  P  V  R  D  B  X  H  W
X  A  F  D  Y  Q  Z  S  M  G  P  D  P  S  F
I  P  D  J  O  U  E  N  L  G  E  E  Z  J  C
H  K  W  T  A  O  G  O  W  B  E  Q  I  N  U
F  B  X  F  D  U  L  I  M  N  H  Y  C  Y  V
M  A  V  A  K  O  X  L  F  Q  S  L  K  P  I
```

CAMEL	EAGLE	LION
CROW	FISH	OX
DEER	FOX	SHEEP
DONKEY	GOAT	SNAKE
DOVE	LAMB	WHALE

2. The Creation of the World

The story of creation is one of the most beautiful in the Bible. God created light, separated land from sea, and filled the world with life. This word search invites you to explore the wonders of creation and find the words that reflect this incredible story.

```
H  W  J  N  Z  V  J  C  I  R  Y  I  H  T  N
E  E  F  S  T  H  I  Y  E  J  L  A  N  D  F
A  L  M  E  D  M  L  I  R  J  Y  I  O  T  B
V  I  O  A  N  E  D  R  A  G  S  J  T  A  E
E  G  O  E  H  X  Z  Q  B  Q  L  F  B  C  T
N  H  N  G  T  S  F  J  Y  T  A  U  Q  J  G
A  T  O  B  R  U  F  X  G  B  M  M  Y  M  E
Q  B  N  A  A  N  S  S  G  N  I  N  R  O  M
A  X  L  V  E  S  A  L  T  Q  N  P  S  T  N
Q  N  E  V  E  N  I  N  G  S  A  L  O  J  P
I  C  P  M  U  H  N  K  D  T  B  A  R  P  X
Q  G  A  D  T  Z  L  O  A  A  P  N  Z  N  D
D  P  A  V  O  Z  K  D  Y  R  Z  T  W  R  T
W  S  N  J  T  Y  Y  H  M  S  A  S  Q  D  W
T  S  Q  Z  Y  N  O  N  S  Z  M  X  S  K  Y
```

ANIMALS	HEAVEN	PLANTS
DAY	LAND	SEA
EARTH	LIGHT	SKY
EVENING	MOON	STARS
GARDEN	MORNING	SUN

3. Famous Heroes of the Bible

The Bible contains inspiring heroes who showed courage, faith, and wisdom. These individuals teach us timeless lessons, from David's bravery against Goliath to Noah's obedience in building the ark. In this word search, find the names of these remarkable figures and remember their incredible stories.

```
I  S  A  A  C  Q  N  O  A  H  E  X  F  N  U
W  E  L  I  J  A  H  P  O  F  S  C  T  M  S
A  P  L  X  Y  I  L  B  G  Y  T  C  C  A  E
L  E  Z  W  M  H  P  L  B  C  H  X  L  H  W
F  U  E  H  O  B  E  J  N  Z  E  O  E  A  F
L  V  J  R  S  M  Q  N  C  E  R  L  I  R  O
O  S  A  D  E  A  S  D  R  U  T  H  N  B  K
C  M  C  H  S  R  L  I  T  Q  T  E  A  A  T
T  S  O  N  K  Y  Y  X  E  K  R  O  D  R  D
S  Z  B  E  H  C  M  L  Z  G  A  E  G  T  D
S  Y  E  R  S  O  L  O  M  O  N  Q  A  C  U
G  H  K  I  H  X  D  Q  X  D  A  V  I  D  A
M  S  B  E  H  E  E  E  V  E  H  A  N  O  J
R  L  I  T  M  A  I  O  P  M  E  R  P  R  G
B  E  J  O  S  E  P  H  O  A  P  D  H  A  O
```

ABRAHAM	EVE	MARY
DANIEL	ISAAC	MOSES
DAVID	JACOB	NOAH
ELIJAH	JONAH	RUTH
ESTHER	JOSEPH	SOLOMON

4. The Miracles of the Bible

The Bible is filled with extraordinary miracles demonstrating God's power and love. From parting the Red Sea to feeding thousands with just a few loaves and fish, these stories inspire awe and faith. Dive into this word search to discover some of the most amazing miracles ever told.

```
A  G  V  P  W  S  E  A  W  F  F  Q  V  L  T
Q  R  H  W  I  N  E  D  T  T  L  N  C  G  H
H  C  Q  G  D  X  T  U  Z  A  A  C  R  K  G
E  U  S  R  E  D  N  O  W  B  Z  F  E  Y  I
A  X  R  E  Y  A  R  P  G  X  A  J  L  V  L
L  S  A  Q  V  M  V  E  M  T  R  O  H  T  G
I  K  Q  H  G  P  G  C  A  I  U  B  T  T  U
N  J  K  D  W  U  I  R  N  F  S  U  O  S  M
G  L  V  H  A  R  P  O  N  M  F  A  I  T  H
Y  Z  O  I  T  O  L  S  A  Z  Q  Y  N  E  E
T  Z  S  Y  E  X  E  S  H  A  A  X  V  H  Y
K  Z  Y  B  R  E  A  D  B  L  I  N  D  P  E
T  Y  A  V  M  H  Y  A  G  N  Y  D  E  O  X
D  U  E  E  Z  U  R  V  Y  G  J  N  S  R  K
L  I  X  S  E  F  I  S  H  R  O  U  I  P  G
```

BLIND	HEALING	PROPHET
BREAD	LAZARUS	SEA
CROSS	LIGHT	WATER
FAITH	MANNA	WINE
FISH	PRAYER	WONDERS

5. Virtues in the Bible

The Bible teaches us virtues that guide our lives and help us become better people. From love and faith to kindness and patience, these values shape who we are and how we treat others. Explore this word search to discover the virtues that make life meaningful.

E	B	Z	B	M	E	X	A	L	Z	H	O	P	E	T
Y	O	J	C	E	C	O	J	K	N	T	J	A	E	B
T	K	X	Y	B	A	P	I	U	L	E	M	E	D	V
T	E	E	E	C	E	Q	Q	F	A	I	T	H	U	G
B	G	X	A	E	P	P	X	E	I	Y	O	E	T	Z
S	A	C	T	H	H	S	Y	F	G	T	W	L	I	W
A	Y	T	I	L	I	M	U	H	G	I	X	P	T	S
C	S	S	E	N	D	N	I	K	A	R	U	A	A	B
Y	R	R	P	P	L	O	V	E	I	A	C	T	R	Q
V	C	W	I	S	D	O	M	M	F	H	O	I	G	V
N	O	I	S	S	A	P	M	O	C	C	U	E	N	H
S	K	F	W	N	Q	C	P	I	O	U	R	N	T	E
V	N	S	R	E	S	P	E	C	T	G	A	C	I	F
M	A	X	H	X	K	U	T	W	S	P	G	E	I	Z
F	O	R	G	I	V	E	N	E	S	S	E	B	P	R

CHARITY	GRATITUDE	LOVE
COMPASSION	HOPE	PATIENCE
COURAGE	HUMILITY	PEACE
FAITH	JOY	RESPECT
FORGIVENESS	KINDNESS	WISDOM

6. Symbols of the Bible

The Bible is rich with symbols that carry deep meanings and spiritual lessons. From the rainbow, a sign of God's promise, to the olive branch, symbolizing peace, these symbols remind us of God's love and guidance. In this word search, find the symbols that bring the Bible's messages to life.

U	R	A	T	S	Y	Q	X	N	E	Y	H	R	O	N
T	W	A	T	E	R	U	B	W	X	C	P	A	F	V
J	F	Z	B	G	X	M	O	O	O	D	J	I	A	D
K	F	M	N	B	L	A	M	R	L	D	B	N	G	S
Y	O	E	C	L	O	R	G	C	O	N	P	B	S	Z
D	B	L	O	K	N	K	H	N	D	X	N	O	T	O
W	B	R	E	A	D	S	R	K	R	H	E	W	O	K
Q	H	O	L	I	V	E	U	V	A	P	T	L	N	B
B	W	H	C	W	D	K	D	N	T	V	P	L	E	G
K	U	T	R	E	Y	S	U	E	L	L	A	M	B	V
R	M	D	O	K	T	A	N	N	A	M	J	L	J	K
F	J	X	S	T	H	L	C	D	O	V	E	V	R	E
W	D	J	S	O	R	Z	T	H	G	I	L	W	F	M
R	F	I	S	H	P	N	C	M	J	O	W	Z	P	K
U	W	B	O	X	K	J	P	S	N	X	X	B	B	F

ALTAR	DOVE	OLIVE
ARK	FISH	RAINBOW
BREAD	LAMB	STAR
CROSS	LIGHT	STONE
CROWN	MANNA	WATER

Maze # 1

Start

End

Maze # 2

Start

End

Maze # 3

Start

End

Maze # 4

Start

End

1. Animals in the Bible

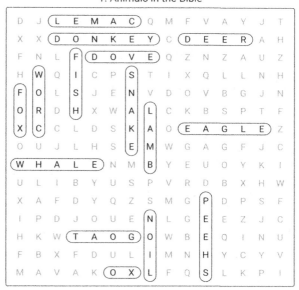

2. The Creation of the World

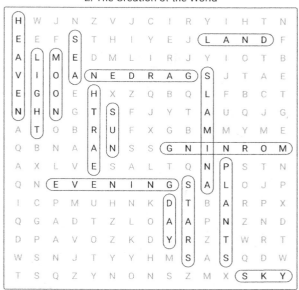

3. Famous Heroes of the Bible

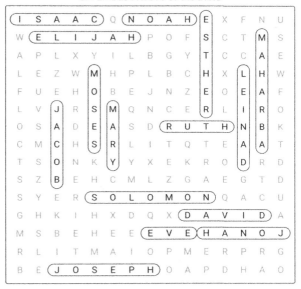

4. The Miracles of the Bible

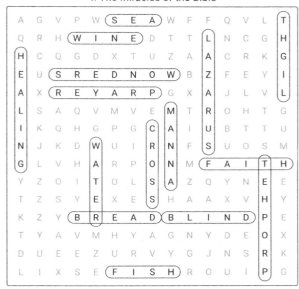

5. Virtues in the Bible

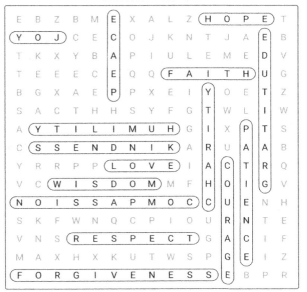

6. Symbols of the Bible

Maze # 1

Maze # 2

Maze # 3

Maze # 4

COLOR TEST PAGE

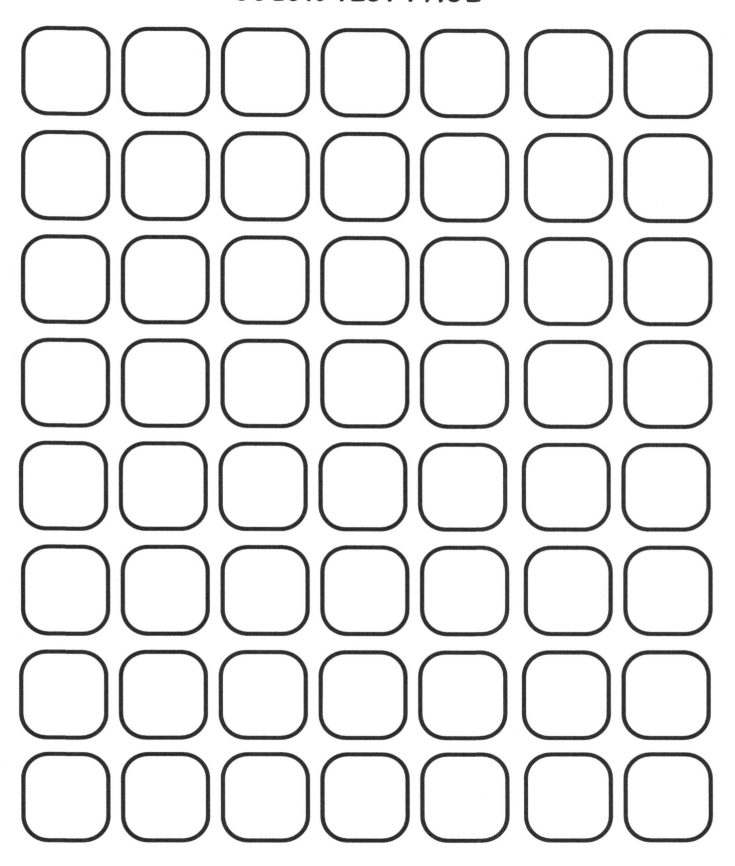

COLOR TEST PAGE

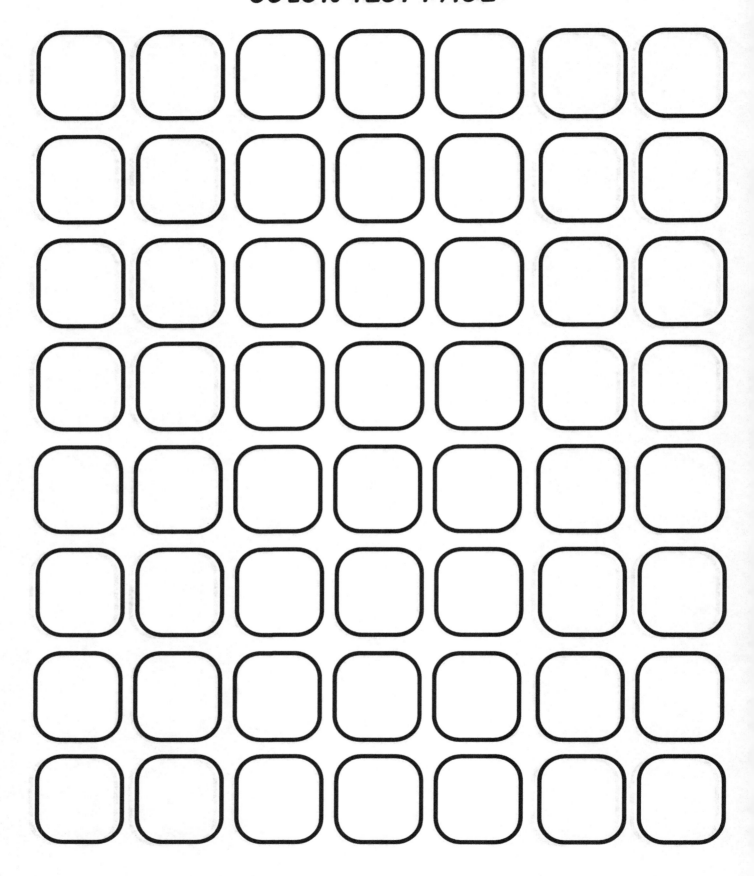

Dear Friend,

Thank you from the bottom of my heart for choosing Bible Story and Activity Book for Kids! It means so much that this book is now a part of your family's journey of faith and learning.

This book was lovingly created to spark joy and curiosity in little hearts while helping them grow closer to the timeless stories and lessons of the Bible. I hope it brings precious moments of discovery and connection between you and your child.

If you enjoyed this book, I invite you to explore more of my hand-drawn creations. Each book is designed with love, care, and a passion for creating meaningful experiences for children and parents alike.

Thank you for supporting my work. It truly inspires me to keep creating for families like yours. I wish you and your family endless moments of joy and wonder!

With gratitude,
Orange Alpaca Press

Made in the USA
Monee, IL
25 May 2025

18125007R00050